Look What Came From the United States

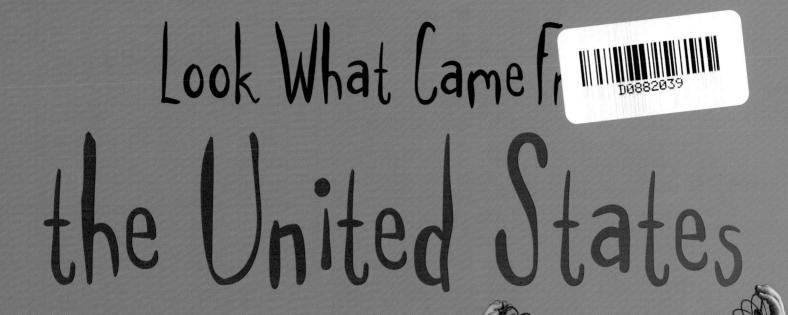

by

Kevin Davis

Franklin Watts
A Division of Scholastic Inc.
New York Toronto London Auckland Sydney
Mexico City New Delhi Hong Kong
Danbury, Connecticut

Series Concept: Shari Joffe
Design: Steve Marton

Library of Congress Cataloging-in-Publication Data

Davis, Kevin A.
    Look What Came From the United States / by Kevin Davis.
        p. cm. — (Look what came from)
    Includes bibliographical references and index.
    ISBN 0-531-11687-5 (lib.bdg.)   0-531-16436-5(pbk.)
    1. United States—Civilization—Juvenile literature.
    2. Civilization—American influences—Juvenile literature.
    I. Title.   II. Series: Look what came from series.
        E169.1.D394   1999
    973—DC21   98-19255
                                                            CIP

Photographs ©: Archive Photos: cover left, 18 right (Herbert), 7 left (Illustrated London News Picture Library), 11 top right (Popperfoto), 7 right, 9 top left, 11 far right, 17 right, 22 right; Corbis-Bettmann: 16 right (Schenectady Museum), 1, 16 left, 19 center, 22 left (UPI), 6, 10, 15 left, 20; Courtesy of Apple Computer, Inc.: 9 bottom right; Craig D. Wood: 4 center; Envision: 25 bottom right (Gary Crandall), cover bottom right, 11 bottom right (D. & I. McDonald), 13 right (Steven Needham), 32 (Osentoski & Zoda); H. Armstrong Roberts, Inc.: cover top right, 3 top, 12 left, 15 center (L. Fritz), 13 left, 15 right (J. Graham), 11 left (R. Krubner), 4 top (F. Sieb), 11 center, 26 bottom (Camerique Stock Photography), 12 right; Monkmeyer Press: 19 left (Sidney); Nance S. Trueworthy: 28, 29 top left, bottom left, bottom right; National Geographic Image Collection: 8 left (Breton Littlehales), 29 top right (Thad Samuels Abell); New England Stock Photo: 14 (John David Harper); North Wind Picture Archives: 18 left; Photo Researchers: border on pages 4, 6-32 (Ken Cavanagh), 3 bottom, 8 top right, 8 bottom right (J-L Charmet/SPL), 19 right (Jerry Wachter); PhotoEdit: 9 bottom left (Tony Freeman); Stock Boston: 4 bottom (Fredrik D. Bodin), 24 right (Tom Walker); Superstock, Inc.: 9 top right, 17 left, 21 bottom, 23, 26 top; Tony Stone Images: 25 left (Stephen Krasemann), cover background (Mark Segal), 21 top (Ron Sherman), 25 top right (Paul Souders), 24 left (Larry Ulrich).

Map by Charise Mericle.

Contents

Greetings from the United States!

The United States is an amazing place. This big and beautiful country is located on the continent of North America, between Canada and Mexico.

Hundreds of years ago, explorers and immigrants from Europe began coming to the United States in search of a better life. The U.S. became known as the land of opportunity. Today, people from all over the world call the United States home.

Long before European explorers came to the United States, the land was occupied by Native Americans. European settlers learned many traditions and valuable lessons from the Native Americans.

The people of the U.S. have contributed lots of great things to the world—let's take a look at some of them!

The flag of the United States

American money

4

Inventions

Christopher Latham Sholes and the first typewriter

Many people use computers to do their typing these days. But not too long ago, people used a machine called a **typewriter.** The first typewriter was invented in the 1860s by Christopher Latham Sholes. His writing machine had a keyboard with all the letters of the alphabet. When you hit a key, the letter would be printed neatly onto paper.

Every time you turn on a light, you are using an amazing invention called the **lightbulb.**

The first lightbulb

Thomas Edison

Edison was a very famous inventor. He also invented the first **phonograph** machine in the 1870s. He used a needle and aluminum foil to record sound. One of his first recordings was the nursery rhyme "Mary Had a Little Lamb." Later, other inventors made discs to record sound and music. Phonograph records are not as popular as they once were. Many people now listen to compact discs, which were invented in Japan.

The first phonograph

It was invented by Thomas Edison in the late 1870s. Before the lightbulb, people used oil lamps and candles to light up rooms at night.

more inventions

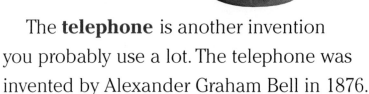
An early telephone designed by Alexander Graham Bell

Do you like to watch **movies?** Edison also made this great form of entertainment possible. His first movie machine was called a **Kinetoscope.** It was a small box that spun pictures around to make it look like the objects in the pictures were moving. In the 1890s, Edison opened the first **movie studio** and **movie theater.**

The **telephone** is another invention you probably use a lot. The telephone was invented by Alexander Graham Bell in 1876. The first person to have a phone at home had no one to call, so he got a phone in his office so his wife could call him there!

Kinetoscope

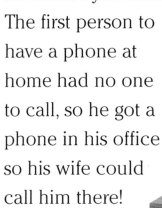
The first telephone

Alexander Graham Bell

Kids using personal computers

The Apple II, the first successful personal computer

A really great writing device that came from the United States was the **ballpoint pen.** People used to dip feathers in ink, which could get messy. In 1888, inventor John H. Loud made a pen with a rotating ball that would evenly distribute ink on paper.

More recently, there have been some amazing

Ballpoint pen

American inventions that have changed the world. One of the most important was the **personal computer.** The first small home computers were made in the 1970s. Many homes and schools now have them. They are much smaller than early computers, which were so big that they took up a whole room! Today, people use home computers for work and play.

9

Transportation

The first elevator

Imagine if you had to walk up the stairs to get to the top of a tall building. It would take a long time and would be very tiring. To help people reach high floors, Eli Otis invented the first **passenger elevator** in 1854. He created a car that had special safety devices so that if a cable broke, the elevator car would not fall down.

Look up in the sky and you'll probably see one of the greatest inventions in transportation history. It's the **airplane!** This incredible flying machine was invented by two brothers from the United States, Wilbur and Orville Wright, in 1903. They learned about flying by studying birds. Many people were afraid of flying, and thought it would never be popular!

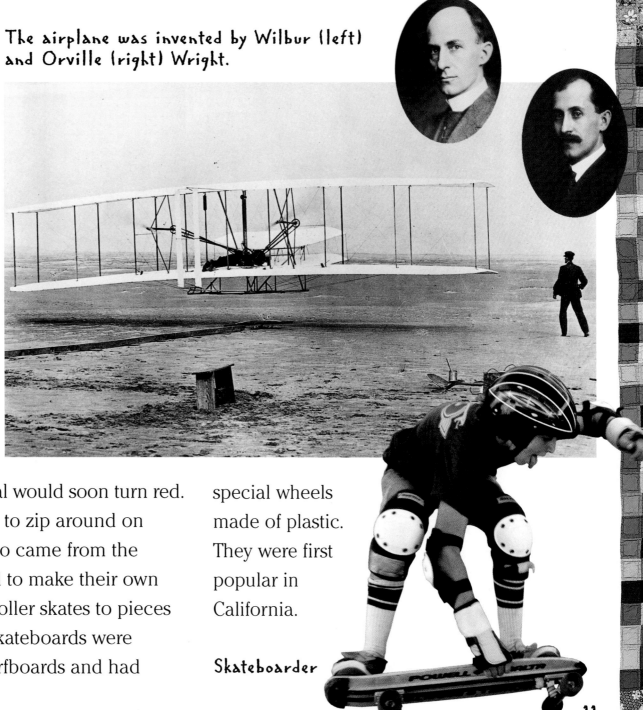

Traffic light

The airplane was invented by Wilbur (left) and Orville (right) Wright.

Although automobiles were not invented in the United States, the first **traffic light** was, in 1914. It had a red light that meant "stop," and a green light that meant "go." Later, a yellow light was added, which meant "slow down" because the signal would soon turn red.

Kids everywhere love to zip around on **skateboards,** which also came from the U.S. Many children used to make their own skateboards by nailing roller skates to pieces of wood. In the 1960s, skateboards were designed to look like surfboards and had special wheels made of plastic. They were first popular in California.

Skateboarder

Food

Popcorn

Corn bread

Many of the foods that are popular in the United States came from Native Americans. Do you like **popcorn?** This fun food was invented by American Indians thousands of years ago. It was discovered when Indians put ears of corn in a fire and it popped into fluffy kernels!

Another food the Indians made first was **corn bread.** They ground corn into flour, mixed it with water and other ingredients, and baked it. Corn bread eventually became very popular in the southern United States.

Pumpkin pie

The traditional Thanksgiving dessert of **pumpkin pie** also came from the Indians. The Indians used pumpkins, a type of squash, in many other dishes, including soup and bread. They also liked to roast the pumpkin seeds to eat as a snack.

Do you like pancakes for breakfast? They're especially tasty with **maple syrup,** which was invented in the United States. Early settlers learned from the Indians that maple trees had a sweet sap that could be made into rich, brown sugar or syrup when boiled.

Maple syrup

Potato chips

more food

Americans invented lots of snack foods, including **potato chips.** This crunchy and salty treat was first made at a restaurant in the 1850s. The chef was asked to make fried potatoes thinner. He made them paper thin, and they got very crispy. People in the restaurant loved them, and potato chips were soon sold everywhere.

Many people used to eat hot cereal for breakfast. Dr. John Kellogg helped start a tradition of cold breakfast cereal with milk when he invented **cornflakes** around 1900.

The baker rolled up thin waffles into a cone and then scooped some ice cream into it. People loved this new way to eat ice cream. Although many people believe that **chili** comes from Mexico, it was really a dish that originated in the state of Texas. It is like a stew, and is usually made with pieces of beef or pork, onions, tomato sauce, and chili peppers.

Ice cream has been around for thousands of years, but an American came up with the great idea of serving it in an **ice-cream cone.** The idea came accidentally at a fair in 1904, when a baker who made waffles was next to a man selling ice cream.

Ice-cream cone

Chili

15

Around the Kitchen

Some of the most popular kitchen appliances came from the United States. The **dishwasher** was invented by Josephine Cochrane in 1886. Cochrane became angry after her servants broke lots of her expensive dishes while washing them. She developed a machine with a wheel that sprayed soapy water into compartments where she put saucers, plates, and cups.

Dishwasher from the 1920s

Do you like to eat toast for breakfast? People used to make toast by sticking bread over a fire. The bread often got burned or did not cook evenly.

The first electric toaster

Making toast became a lot easier when an American inventor designed the first **electric toaster** in 1910. Later, someone put springs in it with a timer so the toast would pop up when it was ready!

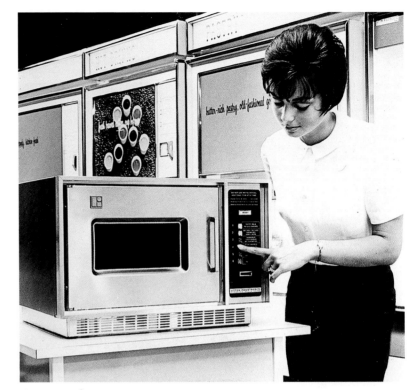

An early microwave oven

Another great kitchen invention was the **blender.** In the 1920s, Stephen Poplawski made a machine with whirling blades that could mix ice cream and milk into a smooth and delicious milkshake. Another man, Fred Waring, also invented a blender, which he used for adult drinks called daiquiris. Soon blenders became very popular.

A more modern kitchen invention from the United States is the **microwave oven,** which was invented in 1952. This amazing device is able to make food hot from the inside out by stirring up the molecules in the food. It can heat up meals in seconds!

An early blender

President Theodore "Teddy" Roosevelt

The first teddy bear

Toys

For thousands of years, children all over the world have played with stuffed dolls and animals. But did you know that the **teddy bear** came from the United States? It was named after U.S. president Teddy Roosevelt. In 1902, a toy maker who learned that Roosevelt liked bears made a stuffed bear which he called the "Teddy Bear."

Silly Putty is a fun toy that was invented by accident. Inventors who were trying to make a new kind of rubber made some that stretched very far. It also bounced very high. They called it "nutty putty." A man bought some, rolled it into balls, packaged it inside plastic eggs, and called it Silly Putty. He began selling it in the 1940s.

Another very popular toy that came from the U.S. in the 1940s is the **Slinky.** This amazing spring is known for its ability to "walk" down stairs. It originally was a metal spring made for boats. When the inventor accidentally dropped the spring, he saw it walk down a shelf, onto a table, and over books by itself.

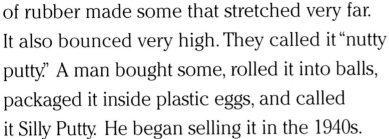

Slinky

Silly Putty

Dog catching a Frisbee

He then let it walk down stairs. His wife thought this would make a great toy.

Have you ever played catch with a **Frisbee?** This very popular flying disc was invented in the 1950s. A man in California made flying discs out of plastic and began selling them as toys.

19

Holidays

One of the oldest holidays in the United States is **Thanksgiving.** Pilgrims, people who came from England to America in the 1600s, began this celebration with the Native Americans they met. Thanksgiving was based on an Indian tradition of offering thanks after a harvest of food. The pilgrims were very thankful to Indians for teaching them about planting and harvesting food.

The first Thanksgiving lasted three days. People brought all kinds of food, including ducks, geese, lobster, clams, corn, vegetables, and fruit. There was a parade, music, and athletic contests. The tradition of eating turkey, cranberry sauce, and pumpkin pie came many years later.

An artist's impression of the first Thanksgiving

One of the most important holidays in the United States is Independence Day, which is also called the **Fourth of July.** This is the anniversary of the signing of the Declaration of Independence, which made the United States its own free country in 1776. Today, people celebrate this holiday with picnics, parades, and big fireworks displays.

Fourth-of-July parade

Have you ever been to a birthday party and sung **"Happy Birthday to You"**? People in the U.S. began singing it in the 1890s. The song was originally called "Good Morning to All," and was sung to schoolchildren. Later, the words were changed to "happy birthday to you." It became a tradition to sing this song at birthday parties just before the guest of honor blows out the candles on a birthday cake.

People singing "Happy Birthday to You"

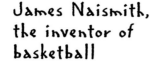
James Naismith, the inventor of basketball

Sports

Early American baseball team

People in the United States are big sports fans. Many of the most popular team sports are based on games that people have played for hundreds or even thousands of years.

One of the most popular sports in the U.S. is **baseball.** It is known as "America's pastime."

Baseball is based on ancient games in which players hit a ball with a stick. It is also similar to an English game called rounders. But a man named Abner Doubleday of the United States is credited with inventing the modern game of baseball in 1839. The United States also formed the first baseball leagues in the early 1900s.

American football is a game that evolved from soccer, which many people in the world

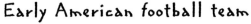
Early American football team

also call football. American football was more like rugby, another game popular in Europe. The first football games were played by college students around 1870. The game is rough, and players wear padding and helmets to protect themselves.

The modern game of **basketball** was invented by American gym teacher James Naismith in the 1890s. Naismith was trying to think of a fun game that students could play indoors between football and baseball seasons. The teacher put up fruit baskets on the balcony of the gym, and players would try to toss the ball into them to get points.

Animals

The **American buffalo,** or bison, is an animal that once roamed the plains and prairies of the United States. This big, shaggy animal was important to the Indians for food and clothing. In the 1800s, many bison were killed by American settlers, but today, the animal is no longer in danger.

American buffalo

The **bald eagle** is a national symbol of the United States, and also was once in danger of becoming extinct. This beautiful bird lives very high in trees and soars through the sky.

Many incredible animals and birds live in the mountains, forests, and deserts of the United States. Some of them were once in danger of becoming extinct, which means that many of them died or were killed by hunters.

Bald eagle

White-tailed deer

Grizzly bears

One of the most common animals in the U.S. is the **white-tailed deer.** It lives in the woods and near cities and towns in many parts of the country.

In the northern part of the country, especially in Alaska, lives the **grizzly bear,** also called the brown bear. These bears usually leave humans alone if not bothered. They have big, sharp claws. When it stands, this bear can be up to 8 feet (2.4 m) tall!

An interesting bird that lives in desert areas is the **roadrunner.** This quick little bird can run faster than people. It sometimes even runs backwards!

Roadrunner

Fashion

Kids wearing blue jeans

One of the most popular kinds of pants in the world were invented in the United States in the 1860s. They're called **blue jeans.** These tough trousers were originally made for workers who needed clothes that did not wear out easily. They were dyed blue so that stains would not show. Soon everyone wanted blue jeans. The first blue jeans were made in San Francisco by Levi Strauss, an immigrant from Germany.

The **zipper** also was invented in the United States. Two different inventors came up with similar ideas for the zipper. The first was called a clasp locker and was invented in 1893.

It was used for boots, but it often got stuck. About 20 years later, a better zipper was invented. It was first used by the U.S. Army for clothes and equipment.

Do you own a pair of **sneakers?** These special shoes, also called gym shoes, were invented in the United States around 1910. Someone got the idea of using rubber on the bottom of shoes, which gave a better grip on the ground. Soon sneakers became very popular with athletes.

Sneakers

To find out more

Here are some other resources to help you learn more about the United States:

Books

Carter, Alden. **The American Revolution: War for Independence.** Franklin Watts, 1993.

Jeffrey, Laura S. **American Inventors of the Twentieth Century.** Enslow Publishers Inc., 1996.

Penner, Lucille Recht. **The Pilgrims at Plymouth.** Random House, 1996.

Sherrow, Victoria. **American Indian Children of the Past.** Millbrook, 1997.

Stein, R. Conrad. **The United States of America.** (Enchantment of the World series). Children's Press, 1994.

World Book Editors. **The American West.** World Book Inc., 1997.

Organizations and Online Sites

The White House for Kids
http:www.whitehouse.gov/kids/
Get a tour of the home and office of the president of the United States, see pictures, and learn the history of this important building in Washington, D.C.

American Memory—Library of Congress Learning Page
http:memory.loc.gov.ammem/ndlpedw.index.html
Pictures, puzzles, games, events, history, and searches of people and places that have to do with the United States.

Plimoth on the Web
http://www.plimoth.org/
Learn about the Pilgrims coming to America, the history of the first colonists, and Thanksgiving. Has links to other historical sites.

United States Environmental Protection Agency Kids Corner
http://biology.usgs.gov/features/kidscorner/kidscrnr.html
Learn about animals and endangered species in the United States, with pictures, history, and a special online animal coloring book.

National Museum of the American Indian
http://www.nmai.si.edu
Facts about American Indians, information about museum exhibits, and links to other sites about Indian history.

A Craft from the United States

Corn-husk Dolls

American Indians have always made beautiful crafts. One group, the Iroquois, makes special dolls from corn husks.

Corn was a very important food for the Iroquois. They had festivals to celebrate the harvest and often made dolls for their children from corn husks. They did not put faces on the dolls, because they believed that only their god should create a face on a being.

Here's what you'll need:

- 8 dried corn husks (soak in warm water before beginning project)
- Towel
- Strong thread
- Scissors

You can dry corn husks in the sun, or you might be able to buy them already dried at a Mexican grocery store.

1. Soak the corn husks in water for one hour so they can be bent and shaped more easily. Then remove them and pat them dry.

2. Get five or six husks and gather them into a bundle. Tie the bundle with thread about 1/2 inch (1 cm) from one end. Make sure you pull the thread tightly.

2

3

3. Fold the bundle of husks in half. Then tie it again about 3/4 inch (2 cm) from the end that is folded. This will be the doll's neck. Trim the other end with scissors so that the entire bundle is about 6 inches (15 cm) long.

4. Get another husk and roll it tightly into a long tube, about as thick as a pencil. Slip this rolled tube under the head, just below where the bundle is tied. Tie another piece of thread under the rolled tube.

5. You can hide the pieces of thread by tying a thin strip of corn husk around them.

4

You can move the arms down toward the doll's body and use thread to tie them. When the corn husks dry, you can cut the thread that held the arms in place.

You can also dress the doll by using scraps of cloth. To make hair, you can glue on pieces of yarn, fabric, or dried corn silk.

5

29

Glossary

anniversary an event that happens on the same day every year, like a birthday

cable a heavy rope, sometimes made of metal

continent one of the major land areas on Earth

contributed to have given something

disc a flat, round object

distribute to spread

evolved came from something else

harvesting picking fruits or vegetables from the land

immigrants people who move from one country to another

introduced brought into use

molecules tiny building blocks that make up matter

occupied to be filled with

opportunity a chance to do or succeed at something

roam to walk around freely

settlers people who move to a new place to live

symbol an object that represents something else

traditions usual ways of doing things

valuable to be worth something

Index

Look what doesn't come from the United States!

Many people like to say something is as "American as apple pie." Even though this dessert is very popular in the United States, both apples and **apple pie** were introduced to the United States by Europeans.

Meet the Author

Kevin Davis is an author and journalist from Chicago. Like many people who live in the United States, his ancestors came from another country. This book is dedicated to his grandfather, Abraham Axelrod, an immigrant who came to the United States from Russia to start a new life and a wonderful family!